Published in Australia in 2023
by Natalie McKenzie
Copyright © 2023 Natalie McKenzie
All Rights Reserved
ISBN: 978-0-6459143-0-6

This book is dedicated to
ALL THE CHILDREN OF THE WORLD.
May we all continue to create a world where children are seen, heard and understood.

Ash Goes to Play Therapy

Natalie McKenzie

Illustrated by Helda Clara

Hi! My name is Ash.

This is my story about going to Play Therapy.

Sometimes I didn't feel good.

I didn't know what to do.

One day my mum told me that:
There are people who help children
when they have worries

and that I was going to see one
of these people.

Mum said that this special kind of person is called a

PLAY THERAPIST.

My Play Therapist's name was Anna.
Anna was nice.

The first time I saw Anna, she showed me a room and told me we would be meeting there every week.

Anna said it was called a

PLAY ROOM.

Anna told me that the Play Room was a special place where I could

PLAY, TALK AND DO MOST OF THE THINGS I WANTED TO DO.

When I was at Play Therapy:
Sometimes I talked and sometimes I didn't.

Sometimes I was quiet.

Sometimes I played alone.

Sometimes I was loud and moved around.

Sometimes I asked Anna to play with me (and she always did!).

I loved being able to
CHOOSE!

It was different in the Play Room from everywhere else.

Sometimes I made a mess.

Sometimes I hit the bag hard.

Anna never got mad or upset with me.

Anna seemed to know what I was telling her (even when I didn't say it in words!).

Anna told me what she noticed I was doing and feeling and most of the time she got it right!

It was like

MAGIC!

Now that I've been to Play Therapy:
I feel happier.

I have more friends.
I like school more.
I try new things.
I have more fun.

I liked going to Play Therapy.
I hope you like it too.

My name is Natalie McKenzie.

I am an Accredited Mental Health Social Worker, Registered Play Therapist, Professional Supervisor and EMDR Therapist.

I currently work as a Private Practitioner in my own business, **Grounded in Growth www.groundedingrowth.org**, and am honoured to be the author of this, my very first children's book, **Ash Goes to Play Therapy**.

I am a passionate Child Centered Play Therapist and have been privileged to work therapeutically with children for over twenty years.

Ash Goes to Play Therapy has been created to help children transition into the therapeutic Play Therapy process with a greater sense of ease and safety.

It is my hope that **Ash Goes to Play Therapy** will be an easy read for children who attend Play Therapy, support the significant people in children's lives to explain what happens in Play Therapy and provide a helpful resource for therapists and other professionals that can be shared with children and families.

Play Therapy provides a beautiful, respectful and deeply powerful opportunity to honour and hold space for the revelation of the wisdom and inner worlds of children and I am absolutely honoured to share this message with you through **Ash Goes to Play Therapy**.

Thank you so much for also sharing this message through the sharing of this book.

With all my love and heart,
Natalie.

Thank you to Yooikagin's team (Helda Clara and Infra Agustin) for working closely with me to create these beautiful illustrations and for helping bring my vision to life.

www.ingramcontent.com/pod-product-compliance
Lightning Source LLC
Chambersburg PA
CBRC092340290426
44109CB00008B/175